Life's Unknowns

Michele Handlir

ISBN: 9798613650507

ACKNOWLEDGMENTS

This is a compilation of personal observations and memories.
Recollections may not be exact. Any errors are unintentional.
Some names have been modified.

Thank you to my family and friends who have
prodded and supported me in writing this book.

1

"Michele...Michele"

"Michele." I thought I heard my name being called out. You know, when you are sleeping soundly and you think you hear your name in a dream, it was like that. Maybe it's part of the dream, maybe it's real—I didn't know and frankly didn't care. I was too exhausted and drifted back into a blissful, sound sleep.

"Michele!" This time, the voice was louder, more emphatic, and authoritative. I brusquely realized it wasn't a dream. Instinctively, I jumped out of bed and rushed to where the voice was coming from—the living room. There he was on the oversized brick-red sectional couch in the living room of our one-bedroom loft apartment, watching television. He was sitting in his basketball shorts, legs up on the chaise ottoman, merino wool hiking crew socks on his feet (his feet were always cold, even in the middle of a sweaty-hot September night).

"I need to go to the hospital. But let's wait until two," he said as I approached, nearly breathless with concern. "Fewer people in the emergency room then," he added. I glanced down at the clock on the cable box, which was perched on the top shelf of the TV stand. In disbelief, I sighed audibly—it was only half past midnight.

"Ok, are you sure you want to wait for another hour and a half?" I asked groggily. "I can take you right now. I'll go get dressed." I turned around to head back to the bedroom, not listening for a reply.

"No, I want to wait until two a.m.," he replied. And he went back to watching an episode of Law & Order. This was his favorite show; he must have seen every episode at least five times.

"Do you want me to sit with you until we leave?" I stopped and said, "Of course." I knew the answer but felt as though I had to ask anyway.

"No," he said, not lifting his bloodshot brown eyes from watching the show.

I was itching to know—why did he wake me up now if his plan was to leave at 2:00 a.m.? I had just laid my head down at 11:00 p.m. I'd been slumbering for a total of an hour and a half, but my head was already very heavy from sleep.

Should I even ask why he wanted to wait? Ok, I was more awake now; I was mildly curious and rather ticked off at the same time. Just ask, I told myself.

"Um, Samir, why did you wake me up now if you wanted to leave for the hospital at two o'clock—in more than an hour? And you don't want any company watching "Doink Doink." I made the funny little Law & Order sound, the Doink Doink, which apparently is rumored to be the sound of a jail cell door slamming shut.

"Just wanted to know you were there," he replied. "Get dressed and go back to sleep. I'll wake you up when we need to go."

"Ok," I said.

What the heck just happened? Seriously, did he just wake me up to "know" I was in bed? Argh. But I'd better do what he wanted. I didn't want to start a fight over something like this, especially when he wasn't feeling well. He'd been having headaches, ranging from annoying to severe, sporadically for the past few weeks. I walked back to the bedroom, switched on the light, opened the closet door, and picked out a pair of jeans and a long-sleeve t-shirt to wear to the emergency room. Those places were always so cold; maybe I'd take my gray, oversized Polo sweatshirt too. I knew I'd be at the hospital for a few hours. Our trips were inevitably a few hours long.

Once I slipped into the shirt and jeans, I laid back onto the bed, atop the fluffy down duvet, and quickly fell back asleep like a log. I was still quite tired. It'd been a long, mentally draining day at work, and I needed a sustained, peaceful rest. Then, in what seemed like just a minute later, I heard it again: "Michele." I knew it was time. As if on autopilot, I headed into the bathroom, brushed my teeth, and threw a bit of water on my face. I'd done this many times before; it was a familiar process. I was ready to brace up for the drive to Samir's preferred hospital in D.C. and the wait once we arrived at the emergency room.

"Do you have everything?" I asked as I ambled barefoot from the bathroom into the dimly lit foyer. I saw he was now dressed in a pair of dark blue Nike sweatpants, a matching tee-shirt, fresh oatmeal-colored hiking socks, and Teva sandals.

"Yes, let's go," he replied. "Let's go *now*." The emphasis was on the word now.

"I've got my wallet, the house keys, the car keys, and my phone," I said out loud, touching each of the items in my purse and running through the list to make sure that I had everything. Still a bit drowsy, I wanted to make sure I had everything because he wouldn't be happy if I had to run back to the house to find my car key or my phone. I asked him, "You have your phone and wallet, right?"

"Why are you asking me? I told you *yes*. Why am I repeating myself? *Let's go!*" He already had his weighty backpack on his right shoulder and was standing nervously, half hunched over, bending his body ever more forward toward the door.

I opened the front door, and we walked out, then down the main stairway, and finally out to the parking lot—all in silence. It was days like this that I wished we didn't live in a fourth-floor walk-up. Luckily, my car was parked in one of the first few parking spaces in front of the building that night. Still in my purse, I pointed the key fob toward the car and pressed the unlock button twice. I heard the clicking sounds of the doors unlocking; otherwise, there was complete silence—no birds, no cars, no neighbors, no conversation. I walked to the driver's side of the car and opened my door. Samir moved to the passenger side and opened his own door. Once we were both inside the car, I put on my seatbelt, put the key in the ignition, and started the engine of his golden-yellow 2001 VW GTI.

"Why aren't you *going*?" he asked somewhat emphatically. Well, it was really more of a statement than a question.

"You don't have your seatbelt on." And, as soon as the words left my lips, I knew I would regret saying them. But it was too late. I could not clutch the words from the air and take them back.

"I don't feel well. *Why are you making this difficult? Just drive!*" Now he was bordering on angry.

"Sorry." That was all I said as I slipped the car into reverse. I just needed to stop talking now. Nothing good would come from me talking at this point.

We drove, in silence, out of the gated Avalon apartment complex, past Tyson's Galleria, then onto Rt. 123. No radio, no conversation, just a few flinches of pain from Samir. I continued to fight the compulsion to ask if he was okay. I knew he wouldn't react well to being asked any further questions. At one point, as we were passing the CIA Headquarters, he said, "Stop driving so fast, or the Fairfax police will pull us over." So, I slowed down from 45 to 40 miles per hour. But there were no police sitting around in their vehicles waiting to catch speeders at this time of the morning in residential McLean, Virginia. I lifted my glasses, rubbed my left eye, and yawned. Hopefully, we'll be at Serenity soon. He was now groaning perceptibly every few minutes and muttering under his breath to himself in Arabic.

Once we crossed over the Chain Bridge viaduct from Rt. 123 onto Canal Road, arriving in D.C., there were other cars around. Yay! Other signs of life at 2:15 a.m. It was only a short ride to Serenity Memorial Hospital once across the three-lane Chain Bridge from Virginia into D.C. It won't be long now. After we were on Canal, it was a left onto Arizona Avenue and then a left turn again onto MacArthur Boulevard. We were nearly there—just a few traffic lights to go.

"*Slow down*. Speed camera, remember?" he said hastily, breaking the prolonged silence.

"Thank you." I replied. I slowed down to 23 miles per hour. The last thing I needed was for him to see the flash of the speed camera to make him even more annoyed.

Samir started to squirm nervously once we neared the final turn onto Loughboro Road. He knew we were close and was ready to be treated.

"*Turn here*," he said. "Drop me off at the emergency room, then park the car."

I knew where to turn. I'd already been to Serenity Memorial Hospital literally a hundred times before. I had come there nearly every day for six months when he was a patient there after his first resection surgery. I'd taken him to the emergency room every few months over the past several years. Yes, I knew the drill. Yes, I knew where to turn. Yes, I knew to drop him off at the entrance. This wasn't my first rodeo. But I suspect that he needed to feel in control of something, especially when he was in this much pain.

We pulled into the circular drive in front of the brightly lit Emergency Room (ER) entrance doorway. When I stopped the car, Samir opened the door and clambered out onto the cement walkway. Without a word, he and his backpack were gone. I reached over, closed the passenger-side door, and drove the car the short distance to the adjacent visitor parking garage.

At this time of day, the parking gate arm was always up, and no ticket was necessary to enter. Fortunately, there were a number of parking spots available near the front exit of the garage. Who else would be parked in the visitor garage at 2:30 a.m.? I pulled into the first empty spot near the entrance pay station. When I let go of the steering wheel to put the car in park, I realized I had been gripping it rather firmly; my hands were nearly numb, white, and oddly misshapen. I guess I was a bit stressed too.

After I gathered my purse from the back seat, I closed the door and started to walk in the direction of the hospital. Truth be told, I enjoyed the short stroll from the visitor parking garage to the ER entrance. It was quite still outside and not too hot for a late summer morning in D.C. The sky was clear, and I could just make out a few bright stars in the sky, even though we were in a major metropolitan setting. I felt a sense of relief wash over me. We were at the hospital, and I could breathe easier. He was going to get the help he needed. I could relax a bit and let the tension go from my mind and body. I could enjoy the stroll in the pre-dawn air.

The security guard at the ER entrance nodded as I walked in. Per recently heightened security measures, the desk attendant asked for my ID as I stepped through the doorway. I grabbed my purse from my right shoulder, set it down on the entryway desk, and fished my ID out of my wallet. Handing my Virginia driver's license to the check-in desk attendant, I explained to her that I was with the gentleman who just arrived a few moments ago—the one in the corner. He was the only person in the waiting room at Serenity that morning.

Samir was slumped over in an old, wood-framed waiting room chair. I'm sure it wasn't comfortable for him sitting on that thin and very worn purple cushioned chair in the far corner of the unadorned waiting room. I strode silently over to where he was sitting. He waved me off. "Don't sit here; sit over there." He sluggishly lifted his arm and pointed toward the other side of the room.

The waiting room was empty. I had my choice of places to sit. It was always the same; we never sat next to one another at the hospital. He said it made him nervous. I chose a seat directly across from where he was seated. He didn't look up; he was busy searching for something in his backpack. Not finding what he was looking for, he let out a profound sigh. "Do you have my phone?" he asked, still rifling through the bag.

"Uh, no." I felt my face flush. "Did you have it in the car?" I knew he did and that he had probably left it in the car. But it was just easier to ask.

"Yes, it's in the car. Would you go get it, *please?*" Now I knew he was really not feeling well. He said, "Please," with sadness in his voice.

Like the agile, sleepy hippopotamus that I am in the pre-dawn hours, I lifted myself out of the chair, nearly tripping on the flat flooring. As I walked toward the exit, I looked back at him and said, "Don't worry, I'll be back in a few minutes with your phone."

"Hurry."

The guard asked where I was heading since he could see Samir had not been treated yet. I explained I'd be back in a minute; I just needed to get something from the car.

Once again, outside of the hospital, I felt a sense of relaxation and peace wash over me as I took in this pleasant morning. But I had to remind myself to walk faster; I was on a mission.

Standing outside the car, I took a deep breath. I grabbed the car key in my purse and clicked the unlock button, just like I'd done a little while earlier this morning. As the overhead light began to illuminate the inside of the VW, I immediately saw his phone in the center console. Whew! One problem solved.

"Just grab the phone and head back"—that was what my inner voice said. Instead, I sat in the passenger seat, dangling my feet outside of the car. I didn't want to be here at Serenity Memorial Hospital again. What was wrong with him this time? A few tears rolled down my chubby cheeks. I wiped them away and got back up. **Be strong. Be normal.**

I walked a bit faster on the way back to make up for the short detour from my mission. I hated walking fast; it hurt my back to walk fast, but the occasion called for it.

Once back inside the ER entrance door, the guard waved me past the desk. I said "Thanks" and gave a wave to the desk attendant.

As I rounded the corner to the waiting room, he was still there. The triage nurse had not seen him yet. I could tell that he was getting more agitated as time passed. "*What took you so long?*" he said in an exasperated voice. As he looked for the phone in my hands, he muttered, "You took too long." I'd been gone for a total of about nine minutes, but who was counting?

"Sorry it took me so long."

"Next time, just be faster." He looked up at me, probably out of habit. As soon as our eyes met, he quickly glanced back down. His eyes betrayed him; I could see he was in pain. "Do you have my phone?" he said with timidity in his voice, staring once more down at the floor.

"Yes, here it is. You were right; it was in the car in the cupholder." I said, extending my right arm to hand the phone to him as I stood in front of him.

"Thanks." He said it with a crack in his voice.

At that moment, I wanted to cry. Luckily, the triage nurse walked over and said she was ready to see him. Samir gingerly got up from the seat and walked with her to the triage room. "Do you want your companion to come with us?" the nurse asked him. "No," he said quietly under his breath. So, I sat down once more in the empty waiting room.

Just a few minutes had passed when I heard "Michele." I was in my own world, halfway between sleeping and daydreaming. The voice was unfamiliar to me. It was a triage nurse calling me. She was standing over the pass-card entry doorway, which led to the ER treatment rooms. After I'd walked over to the doorway, she said that Samir had asked for me to be brought back to the treatment room. She swiped her pass card, and the hefty doors swung open inwardly. "Follow me," she said, as she escorted me to a room in the very back of the nearly empty ward. It must have been a slow night at Serenity. That was a good thing.

I entered the treatment room. Samir was lying down on the bed in one of those threadbare blue and white print cotton hospital gowns that snap up in the back. His sandals were strewn on the floor, but his socks were still on his feet. He seemed to feel less tense now that he was in a room. I walked toward the bed to stand by him when he put his hand up, palm facing me, and said to sit "over there." He then pointed to the lone chair at the far end of the room, under the clock near the door. I did as he asked.

Once I was seated, I sat in absolute silence. I didn't know what to say or what to ask. So, I figured that silence was best. If he wanted to talk, he would. If he had questions, he would ask. If he needed anything, he would let me know. I had to do something to occupy my mind, so I nonchalantly gazed around the treatment room. It was much bigger than any of the other treatment rooms. It had an actual door, not a curtain. This was a proper room, with four walls. One of the walls consisted of four sections of tempered glass with pull-down blinds encased in the glass for privacy. We'd never been in this particular room before. There were all sorts of machines and pieces of equipment covered in thick plastic sheeting in this room. Most of which I had no clue as to what they were or what they did. It felt odd.

We sat in abject silence until the attending doctor arrived. She asked him if it was okay for me to be in the room while she examined him. He was just about to say no when I got up and said that I'd head to the restroom and leave the two of them alone for the examination. (I really did need to use the restroom by this point!) As I headed out of the brightly lit treatment room to the nearest restroom down the hallway, I faintly heard him say that he had a really bad headache, his neck was really stiff, he had trouble concentrating, and it hurt his eyes to read.

When I was finished using the restroom, I washed up and headed back to the examination room, making sure to use the hand sanitizer along the way. There are signs throughout the hallway to use the sanitizer before coming into contact with patients. As I started to walk up the hallway, I could see that the door to the treatment room was closed. There was a big white sign posted on the door and a smaller red sign underneath. My heart started to beat faster, and it felt like there was a lump in my throat. Um, what was going on? The bigger sign read "Isolation—no admittance." The smaller red sign was not easily read from afar, but red is not a positive color for a sign in a hospital.

What had happened since I left for the restroom not even ten minutes ago? I approached the room and just stood in front of the door for a minute, trying to process what was happening. What *was* happening? It was like everything was in slow motion. I kept rereading the signs. Nothing was sinking in. What was happening? I was dumbstruck. Isolation? Contagious? For what? What the heck was going on? My mind was racing; no rational thought was possible.

As I was just standing there in front of the treatment room door, like a marble statue, a doctor walked over toward me. She had on a mask, gloves, and a voluminous suit of some sort. I knew it was serious. Many questions were swarming around in my dumbfounded brain, nearing the tip of my tongue, when she started to talk to me. She hurriedly explained that Samir was in isolation as a precaution. He was exhibiting the symptoms of meningitis. And she went on to explain that meningitis is highly contagious. It was a precaution. No one was allowed to enter his room except the hospital's medical team.

She looked at me for a response or acknowledgement of what she had just said. Some rudimentary understanding from me. I was in shock; my face must have looked completely and utterly blank. She asked me again, as if speaking to a child, if I understood what she had just said. I shook my head up and down; that's all I could do. I could not speak. I was numb, practically paralyzed. And with that, she entered his room and closed the door behind her.

What had just happened? Was I dreaming? This must be a dream, right? Waking up in the middle of the night, driving to the hospital, seeing doctors—I've done all of this a million times before. Maybe this was an incredibly vivid dream, based on previous events. I've had really vivid dreams before. How can I wake myself up? My mind was on autopilot, just breathing. I can't say whether I even blinked at this point. Then I remembered that in the movies, they say to pinch yourself when you think you are dreaming and want to wake up. I'm usually a rational adult, but all rational thought has escaped me at this moment.

I pinched my arm. It hurt! I was awake. This was reality. Samir was in isolation in the ER at Serenity Memorial Hospital. They thought he had meningitis. Meningitis is highly contagious. This was a grave situation.

A nurse walked over to where I was still standing. She must have witnessed the bizarre scene of me pinching myself. She started talking to me, but I couldn't hear her at first. I saw her lips moving; I was looking right at her, but I couldn't hear her. She must have sensed that I was not present with her. She touched my arm and then spoke to me again. It was like a small electrical shock that restarted my internal auditory systems. I heard her this time and could see she had a kind, gentle face with soft, blonde curls falling to the sides. She said I couldn't enter the room. I could "sit outside, in one of the chairs down the hall." They'd let me know what was going on as they knew more, "after his tests." The doctor was going to do a lumbar puncture after she obtained Samir's signed consent when the rest of the team arrived in a few minutes.

I needed to snap out of it!

She asked if I had any questions. Uh, yes, I had questions. I had a million questions and thoughts racing through my head at that very moment. My opening question was clearly not well thought out: "If he has meningitis, then I've already been exposed, so could I just put on a mask and enter the room, please?" She looked at me as if I hadn't heard anything she'd just said.

He was all alone in there. He was in distress. I was absolutely, 100% certain that Samir was in shock at the prospect of that diagnosis, just like I was. I needed to be there with him—for his sake as well as my own. Her answer was a kind yet firm "No." My head was spinning.

When the doctor came out of the room just a few minutes later, she had papers in her hand. When I saw her, I got up from my chair, walked over to her, and asked to enter the room. Her face betrayed a mix of disbelief and annoyance. I said that I'd wear the mask and would sign away any liability for letting me enter the room. She said once the team performed the lumbar puncture, she'd speak to me again. The doctor handed the nurse the paperwork. Just then, some sort of cart was rolled past me into his room. And, with that, the masked and suited-up team, including the doctor, disappeared into the room.

Now tears began to roll down my icy cheeks in a steady, warming stream. I could feel the heat of each individual tear streaking down my face. I possessed a helper personality type, but I could do nothing to help. I felt scared, useless, defeated, and empty. He was the love of my life, and I could do nothing. No, check that; I could pray. But he would have to face this on his own for now.

2

Waiting

The medical team emerged from the treatment room in a burst of activity and noise into the quiet, empty corridor about 45 minutes later. The door shut again behind them with a bang and a click. That bustle of activity continued and sped down the cold, white hallway. It was like a mini-tornado had sprung forth from the room. And then, just as quickly, they were all gone again. Including the doctor.

Could I just sneak into the room without anyone noticing? What could they do to stop me? Would they quarantine me too if I went in? These thoughts and others keep swirling around in my mind. My head now hurt, but I knew the ache was caused by the stress and worry of this bizarre experience. I leaned forward, planted my elbows firmly on my legs, and held my head in the palms of my hands. All I could do was look down at the lightly worn, gray-hued linoleum flooring. There I sat in a solitary blue plastic and silver-tone metal chair in the deserted hallway at the end of the main corridor.

It seemed like an interminable number of hours had passed by. Suddenly, I could sense someone standing in front of me, staring down at me. I raise my gaze partially upward from staring vacantly at the flooring. I could see shoes—a pair of amusingly patterned Dansko clogs. I let out a bit of a giggle. The clogs had a multicolored cheetah pattern. But, to me, at that moment, it looked like a cheetah that had just run through an oil slick. The cheetah print graphic was fashioned in vividly iridescent blues and purples, with a silver snake-like print underlaying certain sections. I needed that giggle.

"Michele?" the person said in a commanding female voice. I wondered how many times she had already said my name to get my attention.

I lifted my head from my hands and looked up. "Yes," I faintly replied. My throat was now very parched, and my tongue felt rough like sandpaper.

"Let's take a walk and talk." The doctor was the same one I had talked to earlier. She must have been the attending ER physician. She started to walk down the hallway a bit, then realized I hadn't gotten up from the chair. "Come, let's take a walk," she reiterated in a more sympathetic voice, motioning for him to come with her.

I rose slowly from the hard, molded-plastic chair. My posterior was numb. My legs felt wobbly too, like colossal molds of beef in savory aspic. I'd been sitting motionless for so long that I was stiff and needed to steady myself against the textureless white wall when I arose. Regaining my composure, I started to walk toward her.

The doctor started to explain that all of Samir's symptoms pointed to a case of spinal meningitis. That's why they performed a lumbar puncture in the examination room earlier. They collected the cerebrospinal fluid (CFS)...something, something, another thing... (she lost me here for a bit) alongside other routine tests, such as blood tests. They sent the CSF she'd collected to the lab to be tested to help confirm or entirely rule out the diagnosis of some form of meningitis. The lab would look at the fluid's general appearance, proteins, white blood cells, glucose, and microorganisms, as well as look for the presence of abnormal cells. And, if I was reading her right, I sensed that she didn't think he had meningitis from the initial fluid she saw. But she didn't want to make that the definitive diagnosis until the lab test results were made available.

"Do you understand what I've told you?" the doctor said.

"Uh, yes, for the most part," I responded. "May I ask you a few questions?"

"Yes, what questions do you have?" she answered.

"When will you know the test results? What are the next steps? Can I see him now?" rolled off my tongue without a breath in between the questions.

"He's resting right now from the procedure. We've given him some pain medication to help reduce the headache and any possible back pain from the lumbar puncture. He has been advised to stay lying down and not elevate his head for at least the next hour." She paused. "We would prefer if you did not enter the room for now, until we receive more of the preliminary test results for other illnesses as well."

I understood what she was saying. I thanked the doctor for her kindness and for taking the time to explain the procedure and testing to me. After that, I said I was ready to see Samir whenever they would allow me to enter the room. I understood the risk and was clear that it was my preference to sit with him as soon as possible.

"Understood. I'll ask the nurse to get you outfitted still, as a precaution, to see him in a few minutes."

My heart was filled with joy. But why? Samir was still in danger. But I told myself, at least I'd get to be with him. He'd know I was there with him, for him.

Soon the nurse came down the hallway with an armful of gear for me to put on before entering the room. "You'd better use the restroom before you put all of this on," she suggested. So I did just that. I made my way to the restroom again and stood in front of the mirror for a brief second. "It will be alright," I told myself. He'll be okay. Be strong. Be normal. With that, I used the restroom, washed up, and threw cold water on my face. "Let's do this," I said to myself. It was time.

After returning to the hallway, I gladly put on the full outfit they use for isolation, as well as the gloves and mask. I was kitted out and ready. There was no hesitation or doubt.

"Ok, are you ready?" the nurse asked as she inspected the outfit front and back, looking at the gloves and mask to make sure I was completely covered.

"Ready as I'll ever be," I retorted with a bit of jocularity in my voice.

"Just remember, *don't remove your mask or gloves at any point while you are in the room.* This is a precaution for your own health and safety." She added, "When you are ready to leave the room, for whatever reason, you'll need to call us. Understood?"

I nodded up and down in an exaggerated fashion and repeated back to her, "Yes, I understand. Don't take off the gloves or mask, and use the call button if I need to leave the room." I understood the risks as well, but I needed to be there with him. Trying to put myself in his shoes for just an instant, I thought, –I wouldn't want to be all alone at this moment.

3

Silence

When the nurse began to open the treatment room door, I could see that there was another, what seemed to be a makeshift, curtained-off area. The curtain consisted of what looked to be a heavier, plasticky version of the same materials as the isolation outfit, giving the area an eerie bluish-green cast. The nurse motioned to enter through the opening in the middle. And, without a word, she closed the door.

I entered through the veil and walked over to the solitary blue plastic chair with silver-tone metal legs in the room. It had been moved and was now just next to the bed on the right side. Slowly, deliberately, and silently, I walked over to that side of the bed. "Samir," I said in a quiet voice, "it's me. They let me come in and visit with you."

He was lying there on his side. He didn't look at me. He stared straight ahead, expressionless and wide-eyed.

After a few seconds, I overheard, "Sit down." His voice was feeble and faint; I barely heard him. He was on painkillers, but that alone did not explain why he seemed so much frailer and weaker than usual. I was startled and sat down almost immediately. He looked so despondent, lying there in that hospital bed, staring straight ahead. What should I say, if anything? I had no real news to give him—nothing that the doctor wouldn't have already shared. And anything I could think to say would sound patronizing and utterly ridiculous. Platitudes like "You'll be alright," "Don't worry," and "It'll all be fine." These were empty, trite, and absolutely meaningless.

Then he asked me a question: "Do you think I'll be okay?"

My heart sank. I was sitting so near to him that I thought he could feel my breath, even through the mask, from the profound and awkward sigh I let out. How could I answer that question? The only way to answer it was to offer him one of those empty platitudes or the plain truth. I'm usually rather cowardly in this type of situation, looking for the easiest way to make someone feel better, happier, and at peace. Suddenly, the words "I don't know" slid softly from my lips. My mind and my mouth seemed to be working independently of one another. "But what I do know is that whatever happens, it's God's will." I added, "If you need anything, just let me know. I can call the nurses for you. If you want to talk or rest, it's up to you. I'll be here." And with that, I fell silent.

"Thank you," he said, and his eyes gently closed.

As I sat there in that blue chair, my mind was again blank, and I suddenly felt very cold. I shivered a bit and rubbed my hands together, forgetting they were gloved. Time passed without notice or indication. He occasionally took a sip of water from a Styrofoam cup with a straw that was positioned near his mouth. But he didn't open his eyes. I fixated on the cup and straw, wanting to make sure they were within reach of his rather parched lips. This was my mission for now: to make sure he could take sips of water. That's one thing I could do for him other than just be there.

Samir groaned a bit as he tried repositioning himself on the bed. My instinct was to say, "Remember not to incline your head," but I fought this urge and stayed silent. He knew he was being careful; he was taking this situation utterly seriously. I wanted to be able to nurse him back to health. But this wasn't about me; it was about him.

More time passed. It's easy to lose track of time in a hospital. Without warning,

I heard someone at the outer door. Samir heard them too. I saw him flinch a tad, but he still didn't want to open his eyes or move. He continued to stay still. The attending doctor entered with a lineup of what I assumed were other doctors. It looked like a scene right out of some dystopian global contagion miniseries. They were all wearing the same isolation gowns, gloves, and masks. You could only tell who was who when they spoke. They introduced themselves, but I took no notice of their individual names, just their areas of specialization. The team consisted of an infectious disease specialist, a rare disease specialist, and the ER doctor. Again, the mood was somber.

It was nearly seven o'clock in the morning. The team had been discussing the tests and results for quite some time. The general consensus was that Samir did not have meningitis. However, he did have something that looked like meningitis, but they were still working on what that something actually was. The doctors began to ask him a barrage of questions: where had he been recently? Had he or any of his friends traveled abroad in the past month? Had this or something like this ever happened to him before? Had he taken any illicit drugs recently? Was he on any unusual homeopathic treatments? And the list continued.

Samir tried, as best as he could, being in such pain, to answer their questions. The answers were all flat. "No." No, he hadn't been abroad. No, he didn't have any friends who'd been abroad recently. No, he didn't do illicit drugs; he took enough prescribed ones. No, he didn't "do homeopathic stuff." And, no, nothing like this had ever happened before. Then there was a moment of silence. I wanted to say, "Tell them you are on treatment for your Crohn's disease." They should know this, right? After all, he took the treatments here at Serenity, just upstairs on the 7th floor at the infusion center. It was hard for me to contain myself, but he was the patient, and he needed to give the information to the doctors. I looked at him, practically willing him telepathically to say something. My eyes were burning a hole in his soul. He opened his eyes and stared back at me. "I'm on a treatment for Crohn's Disease: Remicade."

He had been having a few headaches after each treatment for the last two months. I'd well-meaningly suggested that he tell his gastroenterologist what was happening. But his reaction to this type of suggestion was always the same: "Leave it." This meant, "Leave me alone and stop bugging me about this; if I want to do it, I will." So, I backed off. His health, his treatment, his choices—it was his life, and he was in control.

Samir asked that they contact his gastroenterologist and talk to him about what was happening. Dr. Bulgakov was the only doctor he trusted and listened to regularly. He was more than a doctor to Samir; he was a trusted authority, a person he could consistently go to for help.

The attending doctor said she had already been in contact with Dr. Bulgakov's office, and he was due in the ER to see Samir at any time now. They knew of Samir's underlying chronic illness and that Dr. Bulgakov was his primary doctor. Each time Samir visited Serenity's ER, they always called Dr. Bulgakov's team straightaway. Each visit to the ER could be a potentially life-threatening episode. This visit was no exception, even though the symptoms had no clear relation to his Crohn's issue—not yet.

And as soon as the conversation ended, like ghosts in the night, the doctors glided away through the veil between our world and the other world. We were alone again—together, but alone.

4

Light

Nurses wandered in and out of the room more frequently over the next hour or so. Each making sure he was "comfortable." Seeing if he needed any more water, checking his IV, or taking pain medication. They each asked if he had any numbness or tingling in his legs or had any other kind of distress. They all reminded him to keep his head still and not elevated as much as possible and that he could roll from side to side as long as his head was not elevated. He knew that moving was painful to his head, so he was moving very little at this point. But he really didn't need material; he needed someone; he needed his trusted doctor.

One of the medical team members came back into the room with another nurse. They decided, in light of the test results, to move Samir from the ER to a regular hospital bed upstairs. It was a private room, and he could be isolated for the time being until they figured this mystery out. And Dr. Bulgakov was on his way to the ER; he was in the hospital. There was a nearly imperceptible smile on Samir's pale and tired face. "Ok, thanks," was his reply.

Right after she spoke his name, a member of Dr. Bulgakov's team entered the room through the veil. He was tall and handsome, at least from what I could discern, despite the mask on his face. He introduced himself and said hello, but I didn't process his name. Samir said hello and asked where Dr. Bulgakov was. He said the doctor would be there shortly. He was part of the doctor's gastroenterology team and was just checking in. He wanted to reassure Samir that a "highly qualified team of doctors" was working hard to figure this situation out. And, he added, "They had been conferring with Dr. Bulgakov since early this morning." He added that he'd like to take a few minutes to examine and talk with Samir, if that was possible. "Sure." I knew that was my cue to leave. I'd been in the room for hours. A break would be welcomed.

The nurse and another doctor escorted me to the veiled area in front of the exit door. Between the curtain and the door, we each removed our outer garb and deposited the materials into a touch-free, lidded container that was earmarked for contaminated waste.

Once outside the door, we each went our separate ways. There is much more activity now in the ER. As I glanced around, I could see that more of the white-curtained rooms were now occupied. I heard more voices, saw more movement, and encountered more people. It was a welcome change but disconcerting at the same time. It was great to see people again, hear conversations, and feel normalcy. It was disconcerting to hear the constant beeping and other typical noises of the ER after sitting in relative silence for so long.

Making a beeline for the restroom, I walked in front of the central medical station. There were so many more hospital staff at work at this time of day. Being the partner of a "frequent flier" at Serenity, I recognized some of the nurses and doctors at the station. Accordingly, I nodded and waved to the ones that I knew as I passed by.

Argh. The restroom door was closed. Just as I finished jiggling the handle on the door to confirm it was in use, one of the doctors who had been sitting at the station walked over toward me. She said, "Hello. Nice to see you again, Michele. Is Samir here today?"

"Good morning. Yes, we came in early this morning," I responded, not remembering her name but recognizing her pleasant face. I glanced down at her name tag neatly attached to her white coat to discreetly recall her name. "He's the patient in isolation." I took a breath, wondering if I should say any more to her. But she was a kindhearted, kindred spirit; she was a doctor who was also living with Crohn's. She and Samir had shared numerous stories in the past, so I felt he wouldn't be too uncomfortable with me speaking to her about this issue. "They're still trying to figure out what's wrong with him." I looked directly at her and paused. Then she continued, "They're sending him upstairs soon, hopefully."

"Oh my. I hope he's okay. I know Dr. Bulgakov is usually at the hospital early in the morning. I'm sure he'll be here shortly," she said. "Please give Samir my best. It's always reassuring to see a familiar face; perhaps I can give him a quick wave before he goes up." And then, with perfect timing, the restroom door opened. I made my move toward the restroom and bid her a warm goodbye for now, saying that I'd "pass along your regards to Samir."

As I stood looking in that chipped bathroom mirror, I saw a haggard face. Was that me? I looked like a little old lady who needed a good night's sleep, a phenomenal moisturizer, and some strong coffee. Maybe later today I can catch a quick nap. But, I thought to myself, naps always made me feel groggier and heavier-headed. No, a nap was not going to do me any good, plus there's too much going on to take a nap. I'd had a long day yesterday and no sleep last night. Then, in that instant, I remembered today was a workday. Oh no, I needed to call my office and let them know I wouldn't be in today—well, that I wouldn't be in until they figured out his condition. Dang it, how could I have forgotten all about work? Samir always said, "Work comes first," whatever the situation. Reaching for my purse, I fished out my phone. Without thinking, I unlocked it and dialed up my boss' work line, leaving a message. (I wonder if she could tell by the hollow reverberations that I was calling her from a restroom?) She would hear the message when she arrived at the office in a few minutes. It was already after eight o'clock in the morning. We'd been at the hospital for nearly six hours. It already seemed like days.

On my way back to the examination room, one of the nurses stopped me. She asked if I needed anything—maybe some juice or graham crackers. These were the standard food and drink choices available to patients and guests in the ER. She kindly suggested that I take a few minutes' break, walk around, maybe take a walk outside in the sunlight, and breathe some fresh air. She was right. A break would be refreshing. And I really did need some liquids; I was absolutely parched. My mouth was offensively dry, and I could do with a morsel of food too. "Thank you for asking. Yes, some juice and graham crackers would be much appreciated. You are very kind." She smiled and said she'd be back in a minute. And, within a minute, she was back with a small, sealed orange juice cup and two packets of Keebler Graham crackers. (I have to admit, I love those little Keebler graham crackers you get at the hospital!)

"Why not take these and go for a quick stroll outside? It's a lovely morning, not so hot and sticky yet. He'll be here when you get back; don't worry," she said as she handed me the cup and two small plastic packets of graham crackers. She was right. It would do me good to have a break. I thanked her again for her kindness and decided to take a walk. It would do me good, right?

I truly had no idea I was so hungry or thirsty. The juice was gone before I even made it beyond the medical station. As I passed the station, I started to open the first package of Grahams. I stopped and glanced back over my shoulder toward his room. A searing pang of guilt stabbed my already wounded heart. Without missing a step, I turned around and started to walk back down the long corridor toward the room. By now, the nurse had seen me turning around and returning down the corridor. She could probably read the feelings of guilt on my face. Quickly, she came from around the back of the medical station and met me in the corridor. "Ah, you need another juice; I should have given you more than one; they're so small. Would you like orange juice again, or maybe cranberry or apple this time? And you're lucky this morning; I saw that one of the nurses just brought in a box of donuts. I'll go grab you a donut and another juice. Orange?"

Smiling, I said I could use some apple juice this time and that I'd love a donut. And, just like last time, she returned in a minute, bearing a small plate with a chocolate-glazed donut and an apple juice cup. After she handed them to me, she said she would walk with me to the door; she could use a breath of fresh air too. She motioned to her colleague that she'd be outside and pointed to her watch, then displayed five fingers.

The nurse pushed a button on the wall with her palm, and we stepped through the hefty metal double doors from the ER to the waiting room. Then we turned left and walked through the glass-paneled double doors leading to the outside world. It was a bright, sunny day and not too hot yet. It was early September; it is usually rather balmy and hot in D.C. until after the end of the summer. In that moment, it was slightly jarring to feel the hot breeze caress my ice-cold face. The ER had been freezing. I'd heard that ERs are kept cold to slow bacterial and viral growth, helping to protect patients against contracting new infections or viruses. Maybe that was a good thing. My mind was mushy; my thoughts were scattered.

As we walked together a short distance down the scored cement walkway, the nurse said that she'd need to head back. But she added that I should take a seat on one of the wooden benches for a few minutes and "just soak up the sun and thaw out a bit." She was right. It was therapeutic to be outside in the sun. I sat down, lifted my face up toward the sun, closed my eyes, and breathed deeply, exhaling the stress. Be strong. Be natural.

When I opened my eyes again, she was gone. I glanced behind me toward the ER entrance and could see through the elongated glass window panes that she was in the waiting room, moving hurriedly toward the ER entrance door. How kind of her to encourage me to take a minute for myself and decompress. What a perceptive, caring, and compassionate person!

5

Change

Sitting on that bench outside of the hospital building, even for a few minutes, had done me a world of good. I felt refreshed, invigorated, and renewed. My mind was clearer and more positive. Nevertheless, it was time to go back inside. Once inside the building, I took the long way around to reach the ER. I bypassed the card-access door and headed straight through the lobby toward the back of the ER. When I started to walk down the long corridor toward the examination room that Samir occupied, I could see that there was quite a scene being played out there. Two doctors huddled together with nurses and other hospital staff members. Something was different, though. No one was wearing any special gear. They were all in their normal kit, without special gowns, masks, or gloves.

It looked like they were all preparing to transport Samir to a private room. I continued to walk toward them with a faster gait. I could see the confab was nearing its end. "Perfect timing," I thought as I arrived at the room.

"We're ready," I heard one of the orderlies say. The two doctors nodded, and everyone started to play their part in this scene of this ongoing drama. My part was to play the good-natured onlooker. Someone said, "We're going to room

5E-27."

It all happened so quickly. The next thing I knew, the throng was on its way to the patient elevator and headed to the 5th floor East. After they left, I stepped back into the treatment room and made sure that they had removed all of his belongings. With a bag that had been overlooked and left behind in my hand, I immediately headed to the passenger elevator bank just outside of the ER, where I'd just come from. I knew the nooks and crannies of the hospital quite well by now. How does the saying go: Like the back of my hand? It was an easy trip upstairs to his fifth-floor room.

By the time I exited the passenger elevator, they'd already made their way to the room and had dropped him off. A few of the floor nurses were still assembled outside the door as I walked up. "Hi all. May I go in?"

"Yes. We're just awaiting Dr. Bulgakov's arrival. We've already let him know that Samir has been moved upstairs to this room." And so I stepped inside, hoping to deliver the good news.

When I entered, Samir immediately said, "Sit down. Move my stuff over here so I can reach it." If it were possible, it seemed like he was in better spirits since they'd moved him to a room. It was hard to tell, but he seemed less unsure, more commanding, and more himself.

There was a knock on the door. Samir said, "Come in," but I suspect it was not said loudly enough to be heard outside of the enormous, thick wooden door. Another knock, and the door inched open as the knocking continued. Then the person behind the door spoke. It was a welcomed and familiar voice: Dr. Bulgakov. The doctor strode inside in his immaculately pressed white coat and well-appointed business attire. He always looked very professional and smart. You could feel the change in the room when Dr. Bulgakov entered; it was palpable. Samir seemed to come to life.

The doctor said, "Hi, Michele. Nice to see you again." Then he approached the bed on the side where Samir was facing and said, "Hi Samir, what seems to be going on? I heard you had a rough night." In that instant, Samir seemed to feel more at ease and relaxed. He spoke to Dr. Bulgakov at length about what he had been experiencing, why he came to the ER, and how he felt now, and he even asked how the doctor's family was doing.

"Well," the doctor said, "the test results show that you do not have bacterial meningitis. That's good news. This was a real concern." Other results ruled out parasitic, fungal, and viral meningitis. However, at this point, he said that the disease team is awaiting "further results" from this morning's tests and "may still need to do more testing" to figure out exactly what he did have. Some of the more in-depth results from the morning's numerous rounds of tests would take a bit more time. They will have more answers in the coming hours and days. So, for the time being, he would need to say something in the hospital.

Samir hates hospitals. He hates everything about hospitals. He's spent more time in hospitals than anyone should and has grown wary of them, associating them with troubled times in his life. Normally, he cajoles the doctors and asks why he has to stay in the hospital at all. He didn't even bat an eye when the doctor said he'd have to stay at Serenity for a few days.

Then, Dr. Bulgakov asked how Samir was feeling otherwise—was his Crohn's giving him any issues right now? Somehow, just for today, I think he had forgotten all about the Crohn's disease that he had been struggling with for the entirety of his adult life. He told the doctor that otherwise he was doing well. His belly was fine: no cramps, no unusual diarrhea, no constipation, no recent weight loss or loss of appetite, no swollen joints, no eye redness, or mouth issues. He asked if Samir would mind a quick examination. Yes, this was my cue to leave the room again. Exit stage right.

Once the brief diagnostic conversation and exam were completed, Dr. Bulgakov stepped out of the room, giving Samir a hearty good-bye and letting him know that he'd be back around to check on him later in the day. Once he closed the room's door, he spoke directly to me. "I'll let you know what we find out as soon as we know anything more." I nodded and said, "It is always nice to see you, doctor, and thank you so much for your continued care and attention in all matters of Samir's health." I continued, "I think we were both very shocked and a bit alarmed today by the initial diagnosis. I hope that you find out what's causing his headaches soon."

"We're all working very hard to pin down this diagnosis. I'll be back around to check on him later today before I leave the hospital. There will also be other doctors coming in and asking him questions to help narrow this down." "Ok, so I'll see you later," and with that, he was on his way to see his other patients. I believed in him just as much as Samir did; if anyone could, he would make sure that this mystery was solved. He is a man of rare character and brilliance. He would be an integral part of figuring out what was going on with Samir's health. Samir trusted Dr. Bulgakov with his life.

I tentatively opened the door and walked back into Samir's room. He was still lying on his side, facing the windows. Just as I was about to sit down in a pleasantly fluffy-looking, oversized visitor chair, Samir asked me to take out a textbook from his backpack. Ah, I thought, he's back. He wants to read or do homework. He must want to return to some semblance of normalcy. I wasn't sure if I should even give him a book, given his condition, but I did as he asked. I didn't want to carry out discussions about what he should and should not do. Now is not the time to start an argument. He'd know as soon as he tried to read that he was not quite ready for that leap. And, after thinking it through for that brief second, I fished the book out of his backpack and handed it to him.

As sure as if I had used a crystal ball, he opened the book, stared at it for a minute, and closed the book again. "I've got work to do," he said. "How am I going to be able to get it done?"

"You're not, for now," was my reply. I knew it was a rhetorical question, but I replied anyway, knowing that he actually needed to hear it. "Try again later," I offered in an encouraging manner.

"At least I've got to let my professors know that I won't be in class." He added, "Give me my laptop, please. I need to write a few emails to let my professors know."

"You can do that later; just relax for now. Or why don't you let me type the emails for you so you can rest your head? You just tell me what you want to say, and I'll type it for you. How about that?" In hindsight, that did sound a bit patronizing. But, in my defense, it did seem like a good solution to the predicament at hand.

You could see that he was not pleased with the suggestion; nevertheless, he did see that it made sense for him to dictate and for me to type. He put up the obligatory resistance, but ultimately he said, "Ok, you type. But *only type what I say*. Agreed?" We'd often worked together on written assignments during his undergraduate career and on important emails since then. I'd listen to his ideas, and then I'd compose the written piece. The ideas wound up being mostly his, with a few of my own thoughts and colloquial Americanisms or phrases thrown in now and again. It was perfectly understandable why he was asking for me to type exactly what he said.

"Agreed, only what you say." And with that understanding, we started. We knocked off emails to two professors in the span of ten minutes. There were no major hiccups, and we were working well as a team. I read each email back to him exactly as written. He edited and subsequently approved each email's content. And, ultimately, he hit the send button for each email. Ok, so we were being productive and getting things done together. It was an agreeable and normal few minutes in this otherwise strange situation.

After sending those two emails, he said he needed to rest a bit. His head had started to hurt a bit more again. He said that if I didn't mind, he'd like "to close his eyes for a while." I said, "Of course. Why don't I go to the cafeteria and get something? Then I'll be back in a while."

With his eyes already closed, he said, "You can stay here. I just need to close my eyes. Ok?"

"Ok, I'll stay here. Rest. I'll be right here." I, too, closed my eyes and rested. It felt good to rest a bit. The chair was so comfortable and inviting. I think I fell asleep as soon as I leaned back and my head hit the back of the chair. I was out like the proverbial light.

6

Questions

I'm not sure how long I'd been asleep. I don't think I would have woken up when I did were it not for a resounding knock at the wooden door.

It was the rare disease doctor. She came in and asked how Samir was doing. Then she started a generalized conversation. She went over the previous questions she'd asked him in the early morning. Next, she asked if he ever had any unusual diseases prior to this episode. He replied that he had not—or at least he thought he had not, as far as he knew.

She then said he tested positive for the dengue fever marker, IgG. IgG antibodies were present in his blood work. The doctor went on to say that IgG can be measured for many months and even years after a dengue infection. Samir had no idea what dengue fever even was; he'd never heard of it before that day. So, she explained that it was a virus spread to people through the bite of an infected mosquito. Dengue fever is common in a number of countries around the globe, including some in the Middle East, where a number of outbreaks have recently occurred. She went on to explain that symptoms of dengue include fever, headache, joint pain, rash, belly pain, a general tired feeling, and eye pain. And that there was no specific treatment for dengue. She said it looks like he had the illness years ago; it was not a recent event. So, having said that, she'd ruled out dengue fever as the cause of this current ailment.

Flummoxed, Samir chuckled a bit, smiled, and said he had "no idea about that." No one had ever diagnosed him with dengue fever. This was certainly news to him.

I was smiling a little bit too. What an absolutely crazy situation Samir was in at this moment. Nevertheless, the discovery was a thought-provoking one. It didn't get us closer to the actual cause of the current illness, but it ruled out one possibility. If that's what it took, that's what it took—knock out possible causes one by one.

As they were discussing Samir's bloodwork, the rare disease doctor assured us that they were working diligently to figure this situation out. And anything they uncovered would help inform what it was or was not. So, confirming what I had thought, they were working their way through possibilities one by one.

When she had exhausted the results from this round of tests, the doctor asked Samir if he had any further questions or any information he could possibly think of to help them. He said that he'd told them all that he knew and would let them know if he thought of "anything else that might help."

She let him know that they would need to draw more blood for testing and that they would confer with colleagues outside of Serenity Memorial to help figure this out. They would get him the treatment he needed. For now, though, they would try to make him comfortable, monitor his condition, and keep plugging away to find answers.

This was not a diagnosis, but it was methodical and diagnostic. Samir wasn't overjoyed that there still wasn't a solution, but he knew they were continuing to test and try to find a diagnosis and subsequent treatment.

Talking with the doctor was tremendously taxing on Samir. It took a lot of concentration and strength to use his brain to answer questions and process the conversation. He needed a rest. He still had questions, but they'd have to wait. His tormented brain needed a rest. He closed his eyes and pushed the nurse's call button. Drugs would help him drift off and lessen the pain, both of the headache and the situation. A petite nurse, newly assigned to Samir's room, answered his call and provided a much-needed dose of care, along with his pain medication. It seemed like he was able to doze off for a few minutes. He must have been completely exhausted. I'm sure the pain medication helped with the absolutely overwhelming headache and helped him relax a bit.

The doctors came back later that afternoon. No more discoveries, no more news, no more diagnoses. One moment slipped into the next. Yet again, the hours slipped into each other. It was hard to keep track of the time. Time was beginning to become irrelevant. The present was marked by pain, and the foreseeable future would be too.

Later that night, Dr. Bulgakov stopped by, as promised, to check on Samir. It was again a reassuring visit. And, at the end of the brief conversation, he said he was investigating a theory. He'd know more soon. We were curious but didn't ask any questions. He was acutely aware of the gravity of the situation, and he'd share his theory with us when the time was right.

7

Fear

It had been a hard night. Samir had not really been able to sleep more than an hour at a time and was getting more agitated as time slipped away hour by hour. The next day began much the same as the previous one: a severe headache, a neck ache, blurred vision, an inability to concentrate, and a general feeling of malaise. He was frustrated, in pain, and lacking sleep—a trifecta for a truly bad day.

The morning rounds brought news of other diseases and illnesses that were ruled out. They'd ruled out X, Y, and Z. I stopped paying attention to the illnesses that they had ruled out. Each illness that was ruled out was good news, but not a diagnosis. It was only a matter of time before depression set in.

Samir had suffered from depression ever since I'd known him. He'd had a hard life already, even though he'd just hit his thirties. He'd never really talked about what his life was like with a chronic illness, so I could only guess. I'm sure it was hard. This new illness only compounded his hardship. No one ever got to see the depressed side of Samir, unless he let you. His parents, his younger brother, I, and Dr. Bulgakov were invited into his world to share his illness and his hardships with depression. And, equally, we were all frozen out of his world when he was so inclined. He'd stop communicating his fears and insecurities; he'd tell us less and less about his health; he'd begin to shut us out; and eventually, with all of us at some point or another, he'd just stop talking to us altogether.

I'd stayed the night in his room with him. Hospitals were not meant as places of peace and quiet for resting and getting a good night's sleep. Although I had definitely gotten some shut-eye, I awoke exhausted, hungry, and sore. Without opening my eyes, I sat and let thoughts drift through my weary mind. I wanted to go home to get a shower, brush my teeth, change my clothes, and get something to eat. How was I going to broach this subject with Samir? I had the freedom to leave; he didn't. When he was staying in the hospital, this was never an easy conversation to have with him.

I opened my eyes to the new day to find Samir staring at me. "Ah, you're awake, *finally*," was the greeting of the morning. "I'd like to write a few more emails and try to get some work done."

Thankfully, he's let me get some much-needed sleep. "Ok, but can I use the restroom first?" I said. And with that, I tried to get up. I was slow to get up at first, but then I found my footing. Shuffling across the room on the tops of my shoes, I turned the light on in the bathroom. It was then that I realized that there were no lights on in his room. The bright overhead lights must bother him. I quickly closed the bathroom door.

A good splash of cold water helped me wake up. I used the restroom and adjusted my clothes. Ugh, I really did need to go home and freshen up.

When I left the restroom, I knew I needed to communicate to him that I wanted to go home for an hour or so. Maybe there was something at home he wanted or needed, which would make the fact that I was going to be leaving him alone more palatable.

"Babe, after we work on these emails, I'd like to head home for an hour or so to get a shower and stuff. Is there anything you'd like for me to bring you from home?" My phraseology filter was gone when I was tired, but I tried my best to be earnest and gentle.

"Let's just get through these emails, and then we'll talk."

"Ok, let me get the laptop, and we'll start," was my reply. Sometimes I grew frustrated at inevitably giving in to his desires, but then I'd remember that he was a good person with a hard life and that if I could do things to make his life better or easier, I unequivocally should.

So I took the laptop out of his backpack and handed it to him. He opened it, entered his password, and handed it back to me. It's time to get started.

He dictated emails to a few professors and colleagues at the university. The University of Tennessee Space Institute (UTSI), where Samir studied, is a one-of-a-kind educational and applied science facility. It didn't take too long to finish this up; he had already thought about what he wanted to say. Prepared. He'd been up for hours already, planning for the day ahead.

Once we finished that task, he asked if I'd get him a cup of coffee. Not the coffee they serve on the breakfast tray, but GOOD coffee. Maybe the coffee from the little kiosk in the lobby.

Definitely doable. What time was it, anyway? I'd forgotten to look when I woke up.

It was just after six o'clock in the morning. The kiosk would not be open for another two hours. Life at the hospital would still be in a lull. I explained this to Samir.

"Ok, so why don't you go home, get showered, and then come right back?" He suggested it like it was a new idea all his own.

"Yes, that makes sense. I'll head home for a bit and then come straight back. If you need me, you have your cell; just call me. Or if you think of anything you need for me to bring back, just call me, ok?"

"Ok, but come right back and don't take too long."

"Ok. I'll be back soon." And, with that, I put my purse on my shoulder and headed for the door.

On my way to the elevator, I heard my phone ring. It was Samir. I answered right away. "Everything ok?" I asked.

"Yes, I need a charger for my phone. Please bring one back."

"Ok, I'll bring you a charger. Anything else?"

"No, thanks." The phone went silent, and the conversation ended.

The elevator ride to the lobby floor was a blur. Walking through the administrative hallway to exit the hospital, I started to feel sad and remorseful. I didn't want to leave him. I didn't want to "not be there" for him. I didn't want him to feel abandoned. Once I stepped into the outside world, I felt an immense rush of guilt wash over me yet again. As I walked to the car, I disentangled myself from the guilt. I did really need to leave for a bit to wash up and get his charger, I told myself. I was doing the right thing.

When I arrived at the car, I fumbled in my purse for the keys. Ah, there they were, in the bottom of my bag, amidst candy and gum wrappers, receipts, and a few Kleenex tissues. I used the key fob remote to unlock the car door. I got in, started the car, began to back out of the parking space, and thudded. I'd hit the side mirror on a cement column. Argh. I was just too sleepy to be driving. I put the car into drive and pulled a bit forward, enough to be able to try to back out again. But the damage had already been done. The mirror was cracked, and the casing was scraped. Normally, I would have been devastated and more than a little angry with myself. This morning I was too sleep-deprived and feeling too hopeless to be upset or angry. This was such an inconsequential event that I didn't give it any more thought. I just backed out again, more carefully this time, and left the parking garage for the journey home. I'd change cars when I got back to the apartment complex and forget all about this mirror issue for now. No one needed to be any wiser, especially not Samir.

The trip home was otherwise uneventful. It was early in the morning. I was able to get back to McLean, find a parking spot, walk up the four flights of stairs, shower, brush my teeth, towel dry my hair, put on new clothes, find a charger, put a book to read into my bag, and grab a blueberry muffin from the fridge to eat—all in less than fifty-five minutes. The shower was hot and steamy, helping to wash away the "hospital" from my body as well as my mind. I was on a mission, so I had to keep to the promised schedule. Be strong. Be normal. *Be on time.*

8

News

On my way back to Serenity Memorial, I was ostensibly listening to the news on the Mercedes' radio. Well, I should say that the news channel was playing, but honestly, I did not hear a single word. They could have reported that intercontinental ballistic missiles had been fired and were on a trajectory for D.C., and I would have just kept driving toward the hospital. My mind was somewhere else.

It was a bright, beautiful morning. The sun was shining, the birds were singing, the flowers were blooming, the temperature was in the high 80's F, the humidity was low, the roads were relatively empty, and the traffic lights were all green when I approached. I couldn't have asked for a better day.

As I drove along Route 123, I pressed the button to open the moonroof and wanted to soak up some of that delightful sunlight. The sun's rays were warm and comforting. And, once I arrived back at the hospital again, the temperature in the room would be in the 60s F. I wanted to absorb the sun's warmth before returning to the cold, sterile hospital environment.

In the blink of an eye, I was back in the visitor parking garage. It was a Saturday. More of the spots were filled by other visitors' cars. I did a quick circle around the parking lot's ground level and didn't find an available parking spot. I drove up to the next level and, as luck was on my side that day, found a spot near the elevator. I could feel that today was going to be a good day.

When I arrived at his room, the door was slightly ajar. I gently rapped on the wood, and there was an immediate reply of "Come in." I pushed the heavy wooden door open further. He was in bed with his eyes closed, lights off, shades down, and covered up to his neck with several of the white, open-weave cotton blankets. He was lying on his right side now, facing the door, as opposed to his left side, facing the window, when I left. He'd repositioned himself to see who was entering the room.

I walked in and softly said, "Good morning. I remembered to bring the charger."

"What took you so long? *Did you get my coffee?*"

I'd completely forgotten all about the coffee. Oh, geez. Dang it! "I'm so sorry; I totally spaced out on the coffee. I'll run down to the kiosk and get you a coffee. Hopefully, they are open by now."

"Go now. And come back quickly," he said with a feebler voice.

With that, I pivoted and headed for the door. "Where's my charger?" was the next sound I heard before I exited. I stopped short and fumbled in my purse, saying, "I have it here. I'll put it on your table."

"Plug in my phone."

"Ok, give me a second, and I'll start charging your phone." I plugged the charger into his phone and then into the outlet by his bedside table. "Ok, it's plugged in and charging. I'll head downstairs now. See you in a bit." I continued toward the door as I spoke.

"Just black, no milk, and bring some sugar."

"Yes, dear, just regular black coffee and a few sugar packets," I replied as I left the room.

As I was walking down the hallway, I saw that there were a few more people on the ward now. Rooms were filling up.

Once I arrived on the entry-level floor, I walked through the lobby and stepped into the hallway corridor, all the while hoping the kiosk was open. Yes! It was open. Score! I asked for a large plain black coffee, a large chamomile tea, and a chocolate chip cookie. "Would you like a carrier?" the kindhearted person working at the kiosk asked.

"Yes, please. Thank you for thinking of that. My mind is elsewhere."

"You're welcome. That'll be $7.75."

I swiped my card and reached for the sugar packets. Gripping the carrier, I dropped the sugar packets into one of the open squares and said, "Thanks! "Have a great day," I said as I left the kiosk.

Mission accomplished. Black coffee, hot tea, sugar packets, and a snack.

I walked through the lobby and back to the elevator bank. The smell of the tea steeping was soothing, and the smell of the cookie made me start to salivate a bit. I was looking forward to the pleasant taste of chamomile and imbibing something warm. Of course, the cookie would be great too, but that's for later. Who could tell when the next chance to grab a bite to eat would occur? It's better to stock up and have a snack handy.

As I was making my way back down the hallway, I saw the team of doctors heading into Samir's room. I quickened step by step.

They'd entered the room and were just starting their conversation when I walked in with the treats.

"Put them down and sit over there," Samir said.

The doctors began to go through a litany of other illnesses that they had recently ruled out. More was added to the "it's not" column, but still nothing in the "maybe" or "it is" columns. Samir and I continued to listen intently.

"How are you feeling today: the same, better, or worse?" one of the doctors asked.

"Same"

"Is the pain medication helping at all?" he followed up.

"Sometimes."

"We've already got you on a fairly strong pain medication at a low dosage. Let's up the dosage. We've also started you overnight on general antifungal and viral medication. These should help," the doctor added.

"We're still working hard on this and anticipate having a diagnosis soon. In the interim, rest and let us know if anything changes," the rare disease doctor said in a friendly voice.

"Ok." Samir had kept his eyes shut the entire time the doctors were talking to him.

"We'll check back in on you later." And with that, they left.

"Do you want some coffee now?" I asked.

"Not now, later," was his retort.

"Ok. Just let me know if there's anything I can do," I replied.

I sat back in the comfy chair and pulled out the book from my bag. Then I set my weighty purse on the windowsill above the radiator. I began to read the book in the dimly lit room; fortunately, I was near the window. It was one of the novels in the cookie shop mystery series that I'd recently been reading. They are not noteworthy works of classic literature, but they are fun, easy reads. And, although I don't cook or bake, I love to read about it. And, truth be told, I love whodunit mysteries, so these books are captivating and pass the time.

I'd been reading for maybe two or three hours when there was a knock on the door. It was an odd hour for doctor's rounds. Maybe a nurse? More tests?

It was Dr. Bulgakov.

We were both surprised to see him on a Saturday. "Hi Michele. How are you feeling today, Samir?" he asked.

"Ok."

"Better, worse, or the same?" he added.

"Maybe a bit worse," Samir said.

There was a pause.

The doctor explained that he'd been doing some research over the past 24 hours into a theory he had. He didn't share it earlier because it was just a theory.

"I think we may have a cause," the doctor explained.

Samir opened his eyes wide. "Really?"

"Yes." He went on to explain that he thought it may be a rare immunologic side effect of a drug. Less than 0.1% experience this side effect, which presents like meningitis. He suspected Cytomegalovirus, CMV. He'd already reached out to a few colleagues and the manufacturer of Remicade to discuss Samir's case. They all agreed that CMV may be the likely diagnosis for what Samir was experiencing.

He further explained that CMV is related to the viruses that cause chickenpox, herpes simplex, and mononucleosis. That's why it presents just like meningitis. If you're healthy, CMV mainly stays dormant. People with weakened immunity, like Samir, can experience a reactivation of the virus. Complications of the infection include vision loss due to inflammation of the light-sensing layer of the eye (retinitis) and nervous system problems, including *brain inflammation* (encephalitis).

Dr. Bulgakov went on to explain that he'd already spoken to the other doctors at Serenity Memorial about his findings and ordered a treatment regimen of antiviral medication to aggressively start treating the suspected case of CMV.

Silence.

Silence.

Silence.

"Samir, do you understand what I've been telling you?" He asked in a powerful voice.

"Yes, doctor." There was a pause, and in a very worried voice, Samir asked, "Will I be okay?" Never before had I heard fear in his voice. It sounded like he wanted to cry.

"Yes, eventually you will feel better," he replied with a softer tone. "For now, we need to start you on an aggressive treatment. We'll start you on a treatment with Ganciclovir. Ganciclovir (Cytovene) is the first antiviral medication approved for the treatment of a CMV infection and given intravenously. This is mostly given to patients with the human immunodeficiency virus (HIV). You will need lengthy treatment, and there's no cure for the virus. Improving your immune system is the best hope for combating it, along with the drug therapy."

"I have HIV?" That's the one-word trigger Samir heard, and that petrified him. He nearly stuttered when he said HIV. I can't imagine what was rolling through his mind when he heard about HIV.

"No, Samir, you do not have HIV. The medication we will use to fight the virus, CMV, is used mostly for HIV patients."

"Ok, good." He closed his eyes again. Ok, he didn't have HIV; he'd heard that. Good, he didn't have that. He needed to process all this new information. There was a treatment, but not a cure.

"So, they should be getting you your dose of ganciclovir very soon. I know this is a lot of information to take in. If you have any questions at this moment, I'm happy to answer them now, or you can ask your questions when I stop back," the doctor said.

"Is there anything else I should know?" Samir asked.

"Not really. We just need to get you started on the treatment. And you will need to remain in the hospital until we see progress. I know that no one enjoys staying in the hospital, especially you, but for now it's the best place for you to be," Dr. Bulgakov said in a reassuring, father-like voice.

"Yes, doctor," was his reply.

"Ok, Samir, if you have understood what we've discussed, I'll be on my way and check back with you later." Then he turned to me. "Don't worry," he said, "you can't catch CMV." But I wasn't worried about me catching it; I was worried about Samir's combating it.

"Thank you, doctor. I appreciate your efforts to find out what is wrong. I will do as you advise, doctor. Thank you." Samir said. This was the most he'd spoken in hours.

"You're quite welcome, Samir. I'm just glad we figured this out sooner rather than later. It was a real conundrum," Dr. Bulgakov said as he walked toward the door. He waved to Samir and said good-bye for now.

When he closed the door behind him, Samir waited for a second and then asked, "What is this CMV?"

I re-explained it to him as best I could from what Dr. Bulgakov had said in the conversation a few minutes earlier. Samir was undeniably trying to take in all that had just been told to him; it was just tough for him to think at this point. I suspect he was in shock again, on top of his splitting headache, sleeplessness, anxiety, and general distress.

"I need to rest. Pass me the coffee, please."

"Of course, here's your coffee," I said as I passed him the takeaway cup with the sippy lid. He took a few long sips and handed it back to me.

"Ok, I'll rest for now." And he closed his eyes, pulling the blanket tightly up underneath his deftly bearded chin.

"You rest; I'll be here reading," I said on autopilot. I guess I was going to have to process this information too. What did the doctor mean by "lengthy treatment" and "no cure"? Honestly, I was terrified to know.

9

Treatment

A short time after Dr. Bulgakov left Samir's hospital room, yet another team of doctors arrived to discuss the new treatment. They went over the drug itself, the side effects, and the course of treatment.

The doctors explained, again, that ganciclovir is used to treat the symptoms of Cytomegalovirus (CMV) infection in people whose immune systems are not working fully. They stressed that ganciclovir will not cure this infection, but it may help keep the symptoms from getting worse. A person with a weakened immune system who develops a CMV-related disease (either primary infection or reactivation) will often need lengthy treatment. They discussed how they would monitor his platelet and white blood cell counts during the course of the treatment. They explained that the dosage is based on weight and is done by injection once a day for five days of the week. Lastly, they mentioned that he may experience some of the more common side effects, including a sore throat or fever, nervousness or weakness, or a loss of appetite. The doctors were quick to point out that the virus would continue to cause him pain and discomfort unless checked by drug therapy. So, in essence, there was no real choice in the matter. To slow the reproduction of the virus and eventually perhaps change it to a dormant state again, he would need to take ganciclovir for as long as deemed necessary. And, as Dr. Bulgakov stressed, improving the Samir'sune system was the best hope for combating any kind of invading virus.

Once they finished delivering their monologue about the drug and various side effect disclaimers, they asked if he had any questions. He didn't. What kind of questions was he going to ask anyway? The proverbial train had already left the station. Samir gave his perfunctory permission to start the treatment, and the doctors left the room again.

His first dose of ganciclovir was on its way. At least now the doctors knew what was going on and how to treat the primary illness—the virus. That was a good thing, right? At least Samir was going to get treatment to help ease the headaches and other symptoms. That was a good thing, right? They were going to start an "aggressive treatment" today. That was a good thing, right? So, why could I only hear these two phrases repeating over and over in my mind? "There's no cure for the virus." "Ganciclovir will not cure this infection, but it may help to keep the symptoms from getting worse." Worse? From the outside, his condition already seemed really bad. Knowing it could get worse sent shivers down my spine.

There was no way to read Samir at this point. He had no questions for the doctors, and he had no questions for me. He was completely closed off at this point—walls up, emotions shut down, and communications at a bare minimum. And how could you really blame him? I don't imagine I would have been as stoic and accepting as he was when the diagnosis was delivered. Not knowing what was going on with his health was frightening in and of itself. Knowing just complicated his world a million times over, bringing *another* incurable illness into his life. But, from the outside, he appeared to be taking it in as best he could and to be focusing headfirst on getting better, not on what had already come to pass.

Before we had a chance to settle back and try to talk about the situation at hand, the new treatment medication was here. "I'm ready" was his only utterance before they started. They did a few blood draws before the ganciclovir was administered. Then came the moment—they started the treatment. There was no reluctance, no pause, no sadness, and no emotion. It needed to be done, and he trusted Dr. Bulgakov, so onward he went into the unknown again.

There was no improvement at first. Then, slowly but steadily, he said the headaches were lessening. His blood counts were holding out, so they continued to administer the treatment regimen. Each day the doctors would cycle through his room, discussing the treatment, how he was feeling, and any results from blood work that they had with them. He kept moving forward. They kept moving forward. We all kept moving forward together.

The next few days were a blur. After the weekend, I had to start going back to work. I was unable to take off work completely but was able to divide my time between work and the hospital, sometimes working from the hospital. I tried to spend as much time as possible with Samir at the hospital. He was always so sad when I'd leave. I even tried to sleep overnight in the hospital as much as possible and go home to shower and change clothes before work each day. I was exhausted, but this unquestionably paled in comparison to what he was going through.

I could tell he was starting to feel like the treatments were working because he was more talkative and just livelier overall. He was revived, asking for *real* food, a *real* TV, to catch up on his homework, and to leave the hospital. Mostly, I think he just wanted his ordinary life back.

One day, the long-awaited news was finally delivered: he was going to be released soon. He was ready. Actually, truth be told, he was more than ready! He had been cooped up in that room for days. He wanted out. But it came with stipulations. He needed to continue to take the ganciclovir at home for the foreseeable future. He would need to have a home healthcare worker visit to draw blood for testing and administer the treatment. He would need to take it easy on this brain, meaning not too much reading or studying for now. He would need to rest. He could not drive. He would have to follow up with a pain management center for more drug-based relief from the lingering headaches. And he would have to report in periodically to Dr. Bulgakov. He agreed to all the conditions for release. At this point, I suspect he would have agreed to give up his firstborn to be released from the hospital.

The hospital administrators, nurses, our health insurance company, and I arranged the details of the home healthcare nurse visits, the pain management center's initial consultation, and a follow-up visit with Dr. Bulgakov. The final condition for release was an enormous ask: they discussed how I was to make sure he followed the release conditions. Good luck! Sure, I could influence whether the drugs were delivered, whether the insurance company was actually paying for the care and drugs, when the home healthcare nurse was scheduled to visit, whether the blood tests were carried out on each visit, and the schedule of follow-up visits with doctors. And I could even drive him to all of his appointments. I could influence and affect many of the external parts of his recovery process and treatment. But what I could not be sure of was whether Samir actually followed the rules. He was in control of his behavior. He decided whether he wanted to show up for the visits. He decided whether he wanted to go to the pain management center. He decided whether he felt the treatment was working satisfactorily. He decided if he was going to tell them the truth about his symptoms and overall health, he would conduct the orchestra of people offering help and guidance around him, including me.

The strain of his condition became more evident to each of us with every passing day once he was at home.

10

Challenges

It was a long road to recuperating from the CMV virus. Weeks of ganciclovir treatments, months of pain management, and eventually years of checking on his health.

I was with him through the worst of these CMV challenges. I say I was with him, but really, I was just there for him. It was his struggle and life, and I was there for him to help and support him as best I could. Whether it was sitting by his bedside, getting him a coffee, making sure he ate, typing emails, talking about school, not intruding on his privacy or asking questions, reassuring his parents he was doing better, encouraging him to talk to his parents, taking days off of work, driving him to his appointments, taking road trips with him, dealing with school issues, dealing with unforeseen issues, dealing with the insurance company, engaging a homecare nurse, encouraging him to seek professional psychological help, paying the bills, trying to treat him "normally," or just sitting in silence, I was on the outside trying to make the façade better. He insisted that I treat him like normal, not fuss over him or treat him like there was something wrong with him. He wanted to be normal. But his new normal was anything but normal. Yet, life went on. Each day brought novel issues and trials to our collective patience. What absurd situations were on the horizon?

One day, I received a certified letter in the mail. Neither of us had ever received certified mail before, so this piece of mail with a big green and white barcode sticker stood out. We later learned that the only time people send letters through certified mail is when they want to make sure you receive something, and that something is not usually positive. The envelope's return address was a company in Nashville, Tennessee. With great curiosity, I opened the letter. The letter read, in BIG letters, that this was our final notice. As I skimmed the letter, I saw that a towing company was going to auction off Samir's vehicle on the Monday after Thanksgiving. Any attempts to reconcile the bill would need to be made before the holiday. We received the official letter on Tuesday evening, two days before Thanksgiving.

The letter went on to further explain that the vehicle was being auctioned at the request of the Nashville International Airport (BNA) as collection for an unpaid parking debt. Apparently, Samir had parked his HHR in the Terminal Garage when he flew from Tennessee back to Virginia to seek medical treatment for the CMV infection. The Terminal Garage was the most convenient location to park, as it was attached to the terminal. Of course, that convenience came with a commensurate fee—a parking cost of $20 per day. The Central Parking Corporation and BNA considered the vehicle abandoned after it had been parked in the garage for two months. So, as per their policy, they were moving forward with auctioning off the vehicle to recuperate the lost parking fees, including the towing fee.

I couldn't believe what I was reading. Talk about adding insult to injury. After rereading the letter several more times to absorb the details, I walked over to where Samir was sitting. Handing him the letter, I asked if he knew anything about this. Had there been other letters or perhaps phone calls? This was our last notice; *had* there been a first or second notice?

He responded with the same sort of disbelief I was experiencing. They couldn't auction off his car; it was his, and he'd paid for it completely. He owned it! Abandoned? It was just parked in the garage. In our minds, the airport in Tennessee was trying to literally steal his car.

Unfortunately, it was already after business hours when we were reading the letter. We'd have to take care of this in the morning, the day before

Thanksgiving. You know, the day when most companies give their employees a half day off. This was certainly a new challenge to take his mind off of his illness for at least a few hours. Tonight, there was nothing else to say about this state of affairs. We just needed to make this right.

The next day, I went to work eagerly awaiting the opening of the towing office in Nashville. Promptly at 10:00 a.m. EST (9:00 a.m. CST), I phoned the company. A well-intentioned woman on the other end of the phone explained that they had already sent the car to the auction house, but if I could get there today, Wednesday, with $1,595 in cash to pay off the fees, they could retrieve the car. I explained that we lived in northern Virginia and could not possibly get to Nashville today before they closed. Regrettably, she offered that they would be closed on Friday, so that wasn't an option either. She then countered by telling me that the auction was scheduled for Monday afternoon after the holiday, so if we could get there with the cash before the scheduled auction, we could still have a chance at retrieving the car. But we'd need to be there first thing in the morning. Finally, the conversation ended after nearly forty-five minutes; we'd agreed that they would not proceed with the auction if one of us would be at her office on Monday morning at 9:00 a.m. with the $1,595 cash. She had all of my and Samir's details, including our cellphone numbers, and I had her name, Ruby. We had a plan for tomorrow.

As backup, I then called the Arlington County Department of Motor Vehicles and asked if the title to the vehicle was still in our names. They confirmed that no title transfer had been initiated or requested at that time. I asked them to make a note on the file not to process any such request without our expressed authorization. She explained that their practice would not be to arbitrarily initiate a title transfer and that we would be notified if such an action was requested from an organization outside of the normal car sales channels. Done, or so we thought.

Samir decided to fly into Nashville on the first flight from Dulles International Airport on that Monday morning. When he arrived at BNA, he took a taxi to the towing company's office, arriving promptly at 9:00 a.m., which was in reality 8:00 a.m. in Nashville with the time zone change. He waited at the office door for about an hour until the office opened. Once the office was open for business, the situation began to play out. He asked for the manager, paid her the cash, got a receipt, and asked for his car. She said she'd call the auction house to stop the auction, but that he'd have to actually go there to pick up the car. They didn't open until 10:30 a.m. She had his money, but he didn't yet have his car. With his receipt in hand, he called another taxi and headed for the auction house to get his car back. He arrived just before they opened. Ready with his newly penned receipt and documents, he presented them to the auction house. They promptly called the towing company to verify the documents and their intent to withdraw the car from the auction. The auctioneer's assistant handed the new set of keys for the vehicle over to Samir. They'd had to core the ignition locking cylinder of the HHR since they did not actually have the original keys to the car. Ok, so far, so good, right?

Once he went out to where the car was parked, he noticed it looked clean, like it had just been washed and detailed. This was a pleasant surprise. Maybe this will be a good day after all. But when he opened the car, he realized that all of his things were missing from inside: books, jackets, shoes, sunglasses, and other miscellaneous items. It's great that it was cleaned, but I'm kind of curious that all his stuff was gone. He drove the car the short distance back to the auction house office and walked in to ask about his personal belongings. They explained that all of his personal items had been removed and "recycled." Read: All of his personal belongings had either been thrown away or taken as donations to the local Goodwill Thrift Center. No matter, what was done was done. Chin up; at least he had the car back.

After such a hectic morning, he felt exhausted and energized at the same time. He pondered his circumstances for a minute or two and decided to drive back to Virginia immediately. He called me while I was at work and said he'd retrieved the car. I did a little happy dance. He went on to say that he'd also decided that he wanted to meet at the CarMax in Sterling, near Dulles Airport, later that night to immediately sell the car. That was fine with me; I understood why he'd want to get rid of the HHR now since it had caused such an ordeal, and it felt like the vehicle had been violated. I checked their website and told Samir that CarMax closed daily at 9:00 p.m., so he'd need to hustle. The drive from Nashville was over 650 miles, usually taking between 9 and 10 hours.

The next time I heard from him was at 7:10 p.m.; I was just taking the trash out after dinner to the communal dumpster. He said he was on course to get to CarMax by 8:15 p.m. and that I should plan to be at the location just before his arrival. I immediately went back upstairs, grabbed my purse, headed back out of the apartment door, glided down the stairs, and sprinted for the Mercedes. He might actually beat me there at this time of day. It was normally at least a 45-minute drive from Tysons Corner to Sterling at this time of day. The current forecast for the remainder of the evening is for thunderstorms and heavy showers. I hoped he was okay driving through the rainstorms.

We both pulled into the CarMax parking lot at nearly the same time. I was putting the car in park when Samir called to let me know he saw me and was pulling up beside me. Perfect! He was here; he was okay; the car was okay; things were looking up.

We both made a beeline for the showroom. Full disclaimer: CarMax has been our go-to place to sell our vehicles. We love CarMax! This trip was no different. Once inside, we were pleasantly greeted and assigned a person to walk us through the sales process. Our appraiser was out test-driving and assessing our car in less than 10 minutes. Now, we just needed to wait another 30 minutes until the appraisal was complete and an offer sheet was finalized.

Samir needed a break. He'd been driving like a fiend for hours to get here before the car dealership closed. He was tired and said he had a bit of a headache. He said he wanted to go get a drink from Wegman's in the shopping plaza down the street. We'd get something to eat together afterwards. He clutched the keys to the Mercedes and took his leave whilst the process was ongoing.

True to form, the appraisal came back, and they offered us a very reasonable price for the HHR. Chevy had discontinued manufacturing the HHR, so this was indeed a good price. I told him how much CarMax had offered. His response was "That's great; accept it." He'd been sitting in the Mercedes outside of the showroom, so he simply walked back into the building, and we signed the paperwork. They cut us a check for a little over $10,000. We were both satisfied with the outcome. Despite the outlay of $1,595 for the parking and tow fees, the $94 one-way plane ticket, the $50 in taxi rides, the time and gasoline spent driving back to Virginia, and the general aggravation, we came out on top. It was a good day. He needed good days.

After this trip to Nashville, I think he decided that he would try one last time to commit to continuing his graduate studies at the University of Tennessee. He'd already taken a one-semester medical leave of absence since he'd missed too many classes, deadlines, assignments, quizzes, and tests. When he was in Nashville to recover the car, it seemed from the outside that he had no desire to return to Tullahoma. I was mistaken.

In the end, we were back in Tullahoma one last time. He'd tried earnestly to go back to school. Despite his best efforts, it just wasn't working out. The illness had taken too much out of him. It was too hard to simply read and concentrate, even after receiving treatment for months. He asked me to drive down to Tennessee to pick him up and take him home.

I drove to Tullahoma in two days, stopping for the night in Bristol, Virginia, just at the border of Virginia and Tennessee. Making the drive down Route 81 to the border was just as much driving as I could handle in one day. The drive to Tullahoma from Bristol is beautiful but long. The area around Chattanooga was the best part of the drive. It's a scenic and enjoyable drive. The last leg of the journey on Route 24 is grueling. But once you see Arnold Air Force Base, you know you're close.

As soon as I arrived in Tullahoma, I checked in to the local Holiday Inn Express & Suites for the night. Tullahoma is a small, quaint Southern town. It's a hub for aviation, aeronautics, and avionics activities and industries. Although there's not much to do in Tullahoma, there are quite a few backroad journeys to take in Southern Middle Tennessee, especially if you are interested in whiskey distilleries. Notably, the Jack Daniels Distillery is just a short 20-minute drive away in Lynchburg. Too bad neither of us drank alcohol.

Samir took the car for the night and headed back to the university. He wanted to get started packing up the car with all of his belongings. He was ready to leave early the next morning. After I had a hearty buffet breakfast at the hotel, he came and picked me up. The trip back to Virginia was underway. As we began the journey, Samir asked if I would like to take the short route or the scenic tour on the way home. I opted for the scenic tour, as I always do given the chance. He knew I'd opt for the scenic tour. So, we headed down to Chattanooga, but instead of turning up toward Knoxville, we continued to head down Route 75 toward Atlanta. Skirting downtown Atlanta, Route 85 through Georgia is also a lovely route.

I suspect he secretly planned to take the scenic route because he wanted to pick up a new PlayStation 3D 24" display monitor from a GameStop at the Mall of

Georgia in Buford. The display was a scarce commodity since it had been discontinued a few months earlier. This monster display could turn any bedroom, den, or office into a 3D entertainment haven. Its built-in speakers and subwoofer filled out the audio experience. "Specially enhanced for gaming, SimulView™ technology delivers individual full HD screen action to each player in two-player mode, putting players deeper in the game." This was state-of-the-art for that era. We plotted a course for that GameStop store in the suburbs of Atlanta and successfully completed the mission. He purchased the display, carried it to the car, and loaded it into the back with the rest of his belongings.

After the slight detour, we continued on Route 85 diagonally through North Carolina on the way up to southern Virginia. At some point we stopped at a burger joint along the highway for food; it was all a bit of a blur.

Once Samir and I merged on Route 95, we knew we were just a short two-hour drive from home. He did the majority of the driving on this trip since it was a straight shot. I'd just driven down to Tennessee the day before, so I'd had my fill of driving. It was dark by the time we hit the D.C. Metro region. We were both exhausted and hungry, but we saw the end of our journey together in sight. This was more truthful than we both thought at the time.

11

Broken

Samir said good-bye to his halcyon days in graduate school at UTSI and started to settle back into life in Virginia. While here in the Commonwealth, he had someone who loved him and would take care of him, friends, a welcoming environment, and doctors who were familiar with his medical history. To his credit, he tried everything under the sun to ease his recurring headaches and concentration issues. He continued to see the doctors at the pain management center, as well as Dr. Bulgakov. Often, he'd be home playing video games to mind-numbingly pass the day. Gaming and watching television relieved both the monotony and boredom of being at home with essentially nothing else he could do.

On days when he felt good, we'd go out together. He loved to drive, so on weekends, we'd take road trips through the Virginia countryside. On weekdays, he'd come and pick me up after work at Georgetown University. He'd drive up Prospect Street and wait for me at the intersection of 37th Street. I'd walk down from my office in the Old North Building to meet him "off campus." He didn't want to pick me up at the entrance gate on campus, as he didn't want to meet anyone he knew. After leaving D.C., we'd then head back out to Virginia to one of our favorite restaurants for dinner. We loved to eat out at Wegman's, Chima,

Lebanese Taverna, and Shamshiry. Samir's diet allowed for lots of meat. Raw or hard vegetables were not on the list of approved foods for Crohn's patients. In order to eat vegetables, they needed to be pureed or mashed. Rice was okay too, so Mediterranean food was on the menu a lot.

On days he was not feeling so good, we'd order in from Pizza Movers or another restaurant via GrubHub. We ate far too many beef pepperoni pizzas during this time. The delivery drivers knew Samir by name and his "usual order." Occasionally, we'd sit on the comfy Crate & Barrel couch and watch movies or television shows together.

An aside: This is when we started to watch Game of Thrones together. At first, I hated it. I thought it was some sort of peculiar historical drama with way too much gratuitous sex and violence. But everyone was watching it, and Samir seemed to really be engaged with the show. So I watched it in silence with him on Sunday evenings. Quickly, I learned to appreciate this much-beloved and acclaimed medieval fantasy epic. Its well-developed, complex characters (both loveable and hateable), as well as its remarkable sets and stunning shooting venues, made the show a must-watch for me too.

During this period, Samir would talk on the phone or via Skype for hours at a stretch with colleagues and friends who were living and working back home. This contact was a literal lifeline for him. They'd laugh about something hilarious that had happened recently and tell jokes to one another. Not really understanding Arabic that well and not wanting to listen in, those conversations were mostly private. I was clearly glad he was having some entertaining conversations and laughing. It was good to see him happier and living his life. Yes, occasionally I'd feel a little twinge of jealousy; I wished he'd felt he could joke and laugh with me.

As the weeks and months continued to pass, he'd have good and bad stretches. Days on end, he'd feel well and be prodigious; we'd have fun together. Then, without warning, he'd feel worse again. The good times were great; the bad times were abysmal.

His low times grew more frequent, he grew more irritated, and he grew quicker to anger. I felt compassion for him and his current state. Some days he barely talked at all—to me or anyone else. Some days, I don't think he got up from lying on the couch for hours on end.

Each moment of every day, I was trying to support him by making his life more normal, easier, smoother, and less jam-packed with issues. But, on the flip side, I couldn't treat him like normal. I couldn't get mad at him for being a mess. I couldn't ask how he was feeling. I couldn't leave the house for too long. I wasn't allowed to talk about certain subjects. Did I stumble? Yes. Were there moments when I was frustrated by the situation? Yes. Were there moments when I wanted to throttle him for shutting me out? Yes. Where were the days when I was ready to quit and leave this relationship? Yes. Did I feel like I was being punished for something I didn't do? Yes. Did I keep my composure? Yes, until one day when it was all just too much to bear.

One of the most regrettable moments of my life occurred during this period. I got angry with him one day for the most ridiculous of reasons—it was an outward manifestation of the growing fault lines in the façade.

I don't recall the exact day, but one afternoon I was out at Trader Joe's to pick up groceries. As I was shopping, my mind was elsewhere, and I couldn't remember if we needed more bottled water. He didn't drink water out of the tap; he did not trust the water purification and treatment processes or the condition of the pipes bringing the water to the tap. (As a result, we drank only bottled water at home.) So I called him and asked if we needed more water. He matter-of-factly said, "No, we don't." I asked him to look in the kitchen to make sure. He said he looked, and we didn't. And that was that; the call was over.

When I got home and put away the groceries, I saw that we didn't have any bottled water left in the kitchen. I literally lost it, going from zero to one hundred percent irrational in the blink of an eye. I stormed into the living room, where he was innocently playing a video game, and asked why he had told me we didn't need water when clearly we did. I asked him if he had really checked or just told me that to get me off his back. I was angry and verbally antagonistic toward him, insisting he just should have looked instead of being lazy and fobbing me off.

He quietly stood up and walked around the couch to where I was standing. "Why are you being such a pain?" I asked, "and not participating in this relationship?" A brief silence ensued. "I can't do it all myself!" were my last words before he spoke.

He had just been standing there waiting for me to finish. Finally, he looked at me and started to cry. He was just able to say, "I'm sick; why are you yelling at me?" "I'm sick," he said, and his voice trailed off. His face was filled with wretchedness, and he looked browbeaten. He just stood there.

I was dumbstruck. What had happened to me? Why was I doing this to him? Who cared about the water? I'd finally snapped. I was completely and utterly ashamed of myself. I apologized and explained that this emotional explosion was not even about the water, but that it was about the months of tension and the fear I held in my heart for him. It was about being pushed to the side and feeling unappreciated, uncared for, and unable to help him.

He whispered that he needed "a moment" to himself and walked away.

This was the first time I'd seen him cry. I was so disappointed in myself. He had gone through so much since I'd known him, and a stupid incident over bottled water was my tipping point. I'd made this about me and my feelings. I felt despicable and like I had just gone too far. After a few minutes, he returned to the living room. His demeanor had changed. He was not the same after that.

After dropping out of his graduate program, he subsequently lost his scholarship and, eventually, his position at his employer. It was all too much. At some point, this state of affairs no longer worked for him. He decided to head "back home"—to his parents' home overseas. I have no idea when he decided this or why. He'd actually stopped communicating with me well before this decision. The news was neither anticipated nor welcomed but accepted nonetheless. Our time together was over. Maybe this was what was best for him. Obviously, he'd given great thought to this decision and come up with a solution he thought worked best. He always lived on his own terms and by his own rules. He did what he wanted, when he wanted, and why he wanted. This was no exception.

In hindsight, I honestly think we were both done with our relationship. I confess that before he decided to break it off, I used to mutter to myself, "I can't take this anymore" or "I can't do this for one more minute." From my side, I think I experienced classic "caregiver burnout." I was physically, emotionally, and mentally exhausted. I wasn't sleeping well, and I was always tired. I started to lose interest in going out with my friends. I often felt irritable, argumentative, hopeless, and helpless when around Samir. And yes, at times I felt an unreasonable burden bearing the brunt of his anger, depression, mood swings, and general discontent with his suffering. From his side: I don't know, because he never really shared his thoughts or emotions. Notwithstanding, if I were being completely honest with myself, I'd say it had been broken between us for quite some time. He'd reached his tipping point, and I had too; I was just too afraid to admit it.

Several years later, while he was in the States, Samir called me. When we last met over dinner, he seemed healthier and happier. He'd recently remarried and was expecting his first child. His life seemed to be on a positive trajectory. I was happy for him. From the outside, he looked well, sounded happy, and seemed fine. And, although he seemed to be doing well, his life would still be shadowed by Crohn's disease and CMV. They would always be there, lurking in the background of life's unknowns.

www.ingramcontent.com/pod-product-compliance
Lightning Source LLC
Chambersburg PA
CBHW051231250726
48655CB00006B/2708